IKEDA & IDA: TWO NEW JAPANESE PRINTMAKERS

IKEDA & IDA: TWO NEW JAPANESE PRINTMAKERS

Rand Castile   Japan Society, Inc.

IKEDA & IDA: TWO NEW JAPANESE PRINTMAKERS
is the catalogue of the exhibition of Japan House Gallery
shown in the fall of 1974 as an activity of the Japan Society, Inc.

Copyright © 1974 by Japan Society, Inc.
Printed in the United States of America
Library of Congress Catalogue Card Number 74-13776
ISBN 0-913304-03-4

Contents

ACKNOWLEDGEMENTS	6
LENDERS TO THE EXHIBITION	7
PREFACE	8
IKEDA & IDA: TWO NEW JAPANESE PRINTMAKERS	10
IKEDA MASUO	13
PLATES AND CATALOGUE	17
BIOGRAPHY	26
IDA SHOICHI	29
PLATES AND CATALOGUE	33
BIOGRAPHY	42
FRIENDS OF JAPAN HOUSE GALLERY	44
OFFICERS OF JAPAN SOCIETY, INC., AND ART COMMITTEE	45

Acknowledgements

This marks the first occasion in Japan House for us to present an exhibition of new art, work by living artists, and it is appropriate that we should show prints. This medium has long been acknowledged as one outstanding in Japan, one with a rich history of idea and technique, one that demonstrates the continuity of excellence in Japanese art.

I would like here to express the appreciation of the Japan Society and Japan House Gallery to a number of individuals who cooperated with us in presenting the exhibition; Mr. Aoki Hiroshi of Tokyo; Mr. Suzuki Yoshio of Nagoya who made available for examination and loan his entire collection, a complete assembly of Ikeda prints and an invaluable aid to our selection; Mr. Harry Lunn of Washington, D.C., who commissioned "Venus" and permitted us to introduce the suite; Mr. William S. Lieberman of The Museum of Modern Art and a member of our Committee, whose advice was important in every aspect of the exhibition; Miss Riva Castleman of The Museum of Modern Art, who kindly made available the extensive print resources of the Museum; Miss Shibatani Coco of Kyoto, whose encouragement, advice, and assistance made research an easier task. Finally, I would like to say a special thanks to the artists, Ikeda Masuo and Ida Shoichi whose vision made this show not only possible but necessary.

With the opening of the tenth exhibition at Japan House I would like also to note the sincere appreciation of all of us for the constant support of the Founders and Friends of the Gallery, who, under the leadership of Mrs. Jackson Burke, Chairman, have demonstrated time and again their dedication to the exhibition of the arts of Japan. This program would not be possible without their support.

Rand Castile, Director
Japan House Gallery

NOTE: All Japanese proper names are given in Japanese style, family name first, given name last.

Lenders to the Exhibition

Mr. Kurusina Barunie, Tokyo, Japan
The Brooklyn Museum, New York
Mr. and Mrs. Assa Drori, Los Angeles, California
Mr. Emile Dubrule, New York
Reiko Ehrman, New York
Mr. and Mrs. G. Peabody Gardner, III, New York
Himeji Gallery, Tokyo, Japan
Horie Yasuko, Sakai, Japan
Ida Shoichi, Kyoto, Japan
Ikeda Masuo, New York
Connie Kimos, Kyoto, Japan
Mr. and Mrs. Yale Kneeland, III, New York
Mr. and Mrs. Felix Juda, Los Angeles, California
Miss Alexandra N. Lunn, Washington, D.C.
Mr. and Mrs. Harry H. Lunn, Jr., Washington, D.C.
Maekawa Mitsuko, New York
The Museum of Modern Art, New York
The National Museum of Modern Art, Kyoto, Japan
Dr. and Mrs. Warren I. Pollock, Wilmington, Delaware
Daisy Viertel Shapiro, New York
Barbara Shaw, New York
Shibatani Coco, Kyoto, Japan
Mr. Suzuki Yoshio, Nagoya, Japan
Mr. and Mrs. Gordon B. Washburn

Preface/Ikeda Masuo

In Japan, after the war, a revival of interest in the woodblock dominated the production and sale of current prints. Foreigners were attracted to the images because of their subject matter, which was considered exotic, and because of their colorful and decorative qualities. In retrospect, few of these woodblocks remain significant, and almost none continued the tradition of the authentic *Ukiyo-e* print. With the exception of Munakata, whose major achievement stands in black and white, no single artist fulfilled the promise heralded by the much publicized revival.

The techniques of intaglio printing had been known, and mastered in Japan, since the arrival of the Dutch. The etchings and engravings produced, however, suffered a clandestine existence. Indeed, by the mid-19th century, intaglio techniques were all but forgotten. They were revived, again under European influence, during the second decade of the 20th century. Later, in Paris, Foujita etched some exquisite plates.

After the war, in Japan, a few practitioners of etching and engraving continued stagnant formulas of surrealism which had somehow survived the late 1930's. Hamaguchi, mezzotint master of the still life, unfortunately did not remain in Japan and, like Foujita, became identified with the School of Paris. In 1960, however, etchings by a very young and completely fresh talent began to be seen in Tokyo. They were not well received. It was still the heyday of the woodblock "revival".

In 1952 Ikeda Masuo had moved from Nagano to Tokyo. Born in Manchuria in 1934, he had been repatriated to Japan in 1945. His first efforts at printmaking were woodcuts, illustrations to small precious volumes of verse, which he designed, carved and printed himself. At the age of twenty-two, he turned to intaglio, first etching and aquatint and then drypoint.

By 1960 Ikeda had developed a personal style. A brilliant succession of drypoints often combined etching and roulette to enrich textures and to exploit color with increasing complexity. In 1965, in New York, a selection of his work was collected as a one-man exhibition at The Museum of Modern Art. A year later, Ikeda returned to the United States. At the Tamarind Lithography Workshop in Los Angeles, he learned and mastered another print medium. He has since printed lithographs in Germany, Switzerland, Italy and San Francisco.

The experience of lithography, the most painterly of the graphic media, altered Ikeda's style. In drypoint, his draftsmanship had been an essentially linear, even scratchy, description of form, based upon the outlines of objects. His subject matter was frequently autobiographical and his rendition deliberately naive. In lithography, he developed a more pictorial and modelled representation. On stone and in his later intaglio prints, his description of form is more realistic and often exploits the drama of chiaroscuro.

Paper collage and actual writing had been occasional elements in his earlier prints. More recently, Ikeda uses transferred images in unexpected juxtapositions. He also does not hesitate to borrow from photography as it appears printed in periodicals. He composes in series and each successive sheet unfolds another chapter of some haunted, obsessed dream. His is a poet's revelation, individual, authentic, eloquent. It is fevered by black humor, frank eroticism, and succulent prettiness.

Today, Ikeda is scarcely forty years of age. Before him lies a long career. As did Callot and Piranesi, he continues to work almost exclusively towards printmaking. Like them, he is an exception to the general rule that the best prints are usually created by painters and sculptors.

William S. Lieberman
The Museum of Modern Art
New York

Preface/Ida Shoichi

Ida Shoichi lives in Kyoto. From early work of geometric pattern through recent conceptual prints he has consistently maintained a unique color sense and style. To Ida a multiplicity of prints means nothing more than all things are related.

I first saw his work at Gallery Coco, Kyoto. This was before his extended trip to France. His geometries were printed on both sides of clear plastic, and it was first his colors that attracted me. The same unique color sense is still there and the decisive factor in his prints. It is soft and like a gently hanging veil. The pinks and blues are especially beautiful.

His prints connect infinitely. You can think of his whole work as one print consisting of a multitude of related parts, by implication extending over the whole surface of the earth. And he has wit. And the new work is astonishing.

Nakahara Yusuke
Critic
Tokyo

Ikeda & Ida: Two New Japanese Printmakers

Two hours from here by car Ikeda Masuo is working on a new print. He stays in this country—in a house designed by Hans Noë, set in a forest—about six months a year. He has worked here since 1965 and says it is quieter than Tokyo. His prints have toned down in color since first he came to New York, in fact the recent work is filled with darkening spaces, lots of mezzotint black.

Eighteen hours from here by plane another artist, Ida Shoichi, is at work in Kyoto, the place of his birth. He has just completed a boxed suite of 128 individual prints in an edition of 50. His studio-house is set on the grounds of a temple in the coldest northern region of Kyoto, behind the Golden Pavilion, beside the mirror rock at Takagamine.

Both artists have made their reputations in Japan as printmakers, an ancient and celebrated medium there. Both are young, both men. Neither has been inhibited, constrained, nor weighed down by their country's twelve hundred year tradition of printmaking, a tradition long on technique and usually demanding of an artist that he adhere to the lines of history.

After Hiroshige (Ichiryusai Hiroshige, 1797-1858) Japanese printmaking went through a difficult period of adjustment to foreign influences; perspective, new pigments, different papers, new subjects, each influenced the artists of the time and wrought change upon the whole structure of the Japanese print. This change did not always contribute to a higher order of prints or better use of the medium.

It was not until much later—about the middle twenties and early thirties of this century—that newly introduced elements settled down in the eye of the Japanese artist to produce an unselfconscious, unawkward image best shown in the work of Munakata Shiko and Hiratsuka Un'ichi, where idea, technique and surface are at perfect ease.

Because Japan was closed to any outside influence during the Tokugawa rule (1615-1868) much had been made recently of the *soi-disant* Westernization of that country. Visitors to Tokyo deplore the tall buildings which dominate the Tokyo cityscape, as though Japan had no right to the twentieth century. There is little that is Western about a crowded city having to stack offices one atop another; it is in the nature of an urban setting, East or West.

It is in the nature of an active artist to perceive what it is that best serves his vision. That his history in Japan is older than others', that there is a distinct edge to his culture at home makes contemporary technique—technique is, after all, available—no less his than any other's. He will do what he must do.

Contemporary Japanese art stands on its own as a national entity with international implications. Having mastered techniques not original to Japan the artists there have long been free to participate on their own terms with others in the international arena of competition and exhibition. And they have done well. The printmakers in this exhibition have many international exhibitions to their credit.

Ikeda Masuo was born in Manchuria forty years ago. Ida Shoichi was born in Kyoto thirty-three years ago. Ikeda is largely self-taught, having been refused admission to Tokyo's famed arts college. Ida is highly educated in the medium, a graduate of Kyoto's arts college, at which he taught for a number of semesters.

Kanto—the area around Tokyo—and Kansai—the Kyoto area—have traditionally been rivals for the claim of art capital of Japan. Tokyo, vastly larger, newer, is justly regarded as the capital of new art; Kyoto—with thousands of temples and shrines and gardens—remains the center of tradition. But increasingly place plays less and less a role in a Japanese printmaker's image; neither man is so much an exile from the traditions of his land as an internationalist. Between them they have altered the state of printmaking in Japan. They stand in sharp contrast; it is their collective work, together with their contemporaries (Ay-O, Noda, Yokoo, Kurosaki, Yoshihara), which makes the medium a vital and important one today.

Unlike European and American artists, the printmakers in Japan are first and foremost printmakers, not artists whose reputations are based in another medium—painting, sculpture—who turn to prints for an extension of expression. This is one aspect of their career which is Japanese; with few exceptions (Yoshihara Jiro, Takamatsu Jiro, Onosato Toshinobu) printmakers in Japan are not also painters or sculptors. Aside from Yoshihara Jiro, rarely has a contemporary painter there produced important prints. There is no Japanese Jasper Johns. Perhaps this is an influence of tradition in a nation where for centuries an artist could be as important in reputation as a printmaker as another could be as a painter; Kitagawa Utamaro ranks with Kano Tanyu, Suzuki Harunobu with Sakai Hoitsu.

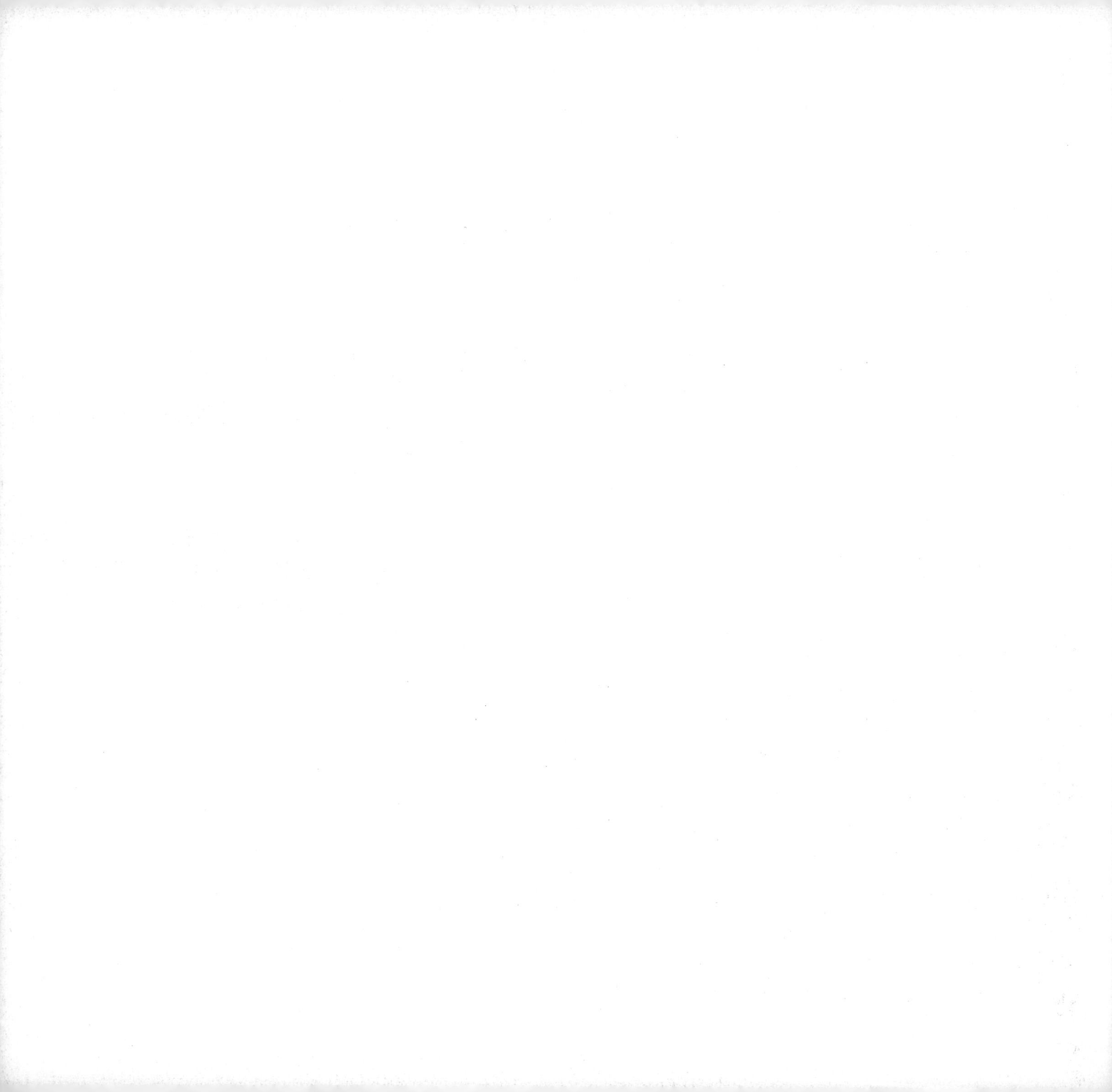

IKEDA MASUO

Ikeda Masuo

Ka, ki, ku, ke, ko; by the *kana* syllabaries Ikeda comes first; he is oldest and by tradition should come first. He is also the better known of the two artists in the exhibition, being the recipient of the International Grand Prize of the Venice Biennale in graphics, 1966, and the subject of the first one man show of an Asian artist in the main galleries at The Museum of Modern Art, New York, 1965. His biography and a catalogue *raisonné* have already been published.

Born in Manchuria, 1934, repatriated to the homeland of his father, Nagano Prefecture, in 1945, Ikeda moved to Tokyo in 1952. Having been refused admission to the arts college he set off on his own to master the print discipline while painting. He showed first his oils at Form Gallery in 1956, the year he began the study of etching at the suggestion of Ei-Kyu. But oil for him was an unsatisfactory medium; much repainting, retouching, piling up of surface bored him. He wanted a medium that would let his hand have its habits with line.

The first prints in this technique he made to sell. He needed money, and after a while he did sell. These were partly abstract, partly figurative, nervous with line and form. In 1958 he returned to an earlier figurative depiction with great success in "Two Ladies" and "My Virgin". Here he begins to find himself and sweeps through 1959 and 1960 with strongly drawn women in etching and dry point.

1962 marks the beginning of his prints that were to be internationally acclaimed through exhibition at The Museum of Modern Art, New York, and elsewhere. These predominantly figurative works were in etching, dry point, roulette, light in color, complicated in surface, often witty. His mastery of technique was complete. He had found a vision.

He has said he wanted to give a special language to familiar things, draw upon the available and everyday. This is evident in the scrawled words, parts of words, letters, numbers, and signs that proliferate in work of the period. Much of this is mirror writing and occasionally important to read, such as in "Romantic Scene", 1965, where some favorite artists are listed (Wols, Dubuffet, Giacometti, Klee, Gauguin, Rousseau, and others). Not one Japanese name here, perhaps because it was literature, not painting or printmaking, that most influenced Ikeda. He is, in fact, a prolific writer, publishing essays, autobiographic statements, and reports from his travels regularly. He is intensely literary himself in the tradition of the *Bunjin-ga.* He is also active in designing and hand printing books; see the miniature book in this exhibition.

In 1966 at the suggestion of William S. Lieberman of The Museum of Modern Art, Ikeda took up lithography at the Tamarind Workshop in Los Angeles. This marked a dramatic change in his work and occurred at about the time of his grand prize at the Venice Biennale, which itself followed the award of a Japan Society fellowship the same year.

From this point he developed an explicitness in his work, a downplay of the humor so important earlier, a simplification of color elements as planes against which women, animals, and objects took form. He gets his clues from magazines—mostly fashion or girlie—newspapers, typography, and photography. Things are more clearly seen than before but no less enigmatic or titillating. He learned a casual and graceful collage technique and applied the results to the stone. In September of 1970 he completed what may stand to date as his master folio: "Portrait of Sphinx", six intaglios commissioned by Associated American Artists, New York. This is a splendidly controlled and colored series of Western women—most of his printed women are Western.

Of large importance to Ikeda's recent work is a return to watercolor as a medium, and now one can see constant reference in his prints to the inspiration of the light brush with its immediacy, flowing color, unlabored effect. In a forthcoming book, "My Imagination Map", Ikeda traces the development of his prints by matching each with a drawing or watercolor study. The nervous line, word landscape, eroticism, complication of form—all are found clearly present in his drawings. It can in fact be said that many of Ikeda's ideas are more clearly stated in these drawings than in the prints, perhaps deliberately muted in his until-now more public medium of etching or lithograph. Rampant eroticism—as in many of the best of the traditional Japanese printmakers—is everywhere evident.

Ikeda's prints are concerned in their image with simple themes, everyday objects, friends, lovers, breakfast, sheep, words, coats, chairs, but these are expressed in a most subtle, complicated, intricately wrought technique. What he wants to say is not of moment, but of the moment.

His early and unusual acclaim abroad might have precluded acceptance at home—as has often been the case with Japanese artists—but this did not happen. The exception in his case perhaps lies in his ability to write for Japanese magazines, developing a rapport with colleagues at home. This and his frequent returns to Tokyo kept him free from the rancor that attends one whose first great successes are abroad.

In the seven hundred prints Ikeda has created to date we see a brilliance of idea and execution perhaps unmatched in Japan today. He is a rightful inheritor of his country's great tradition of awesome genius in the medium. He richly deserves the international acclaim that is sure to continue.

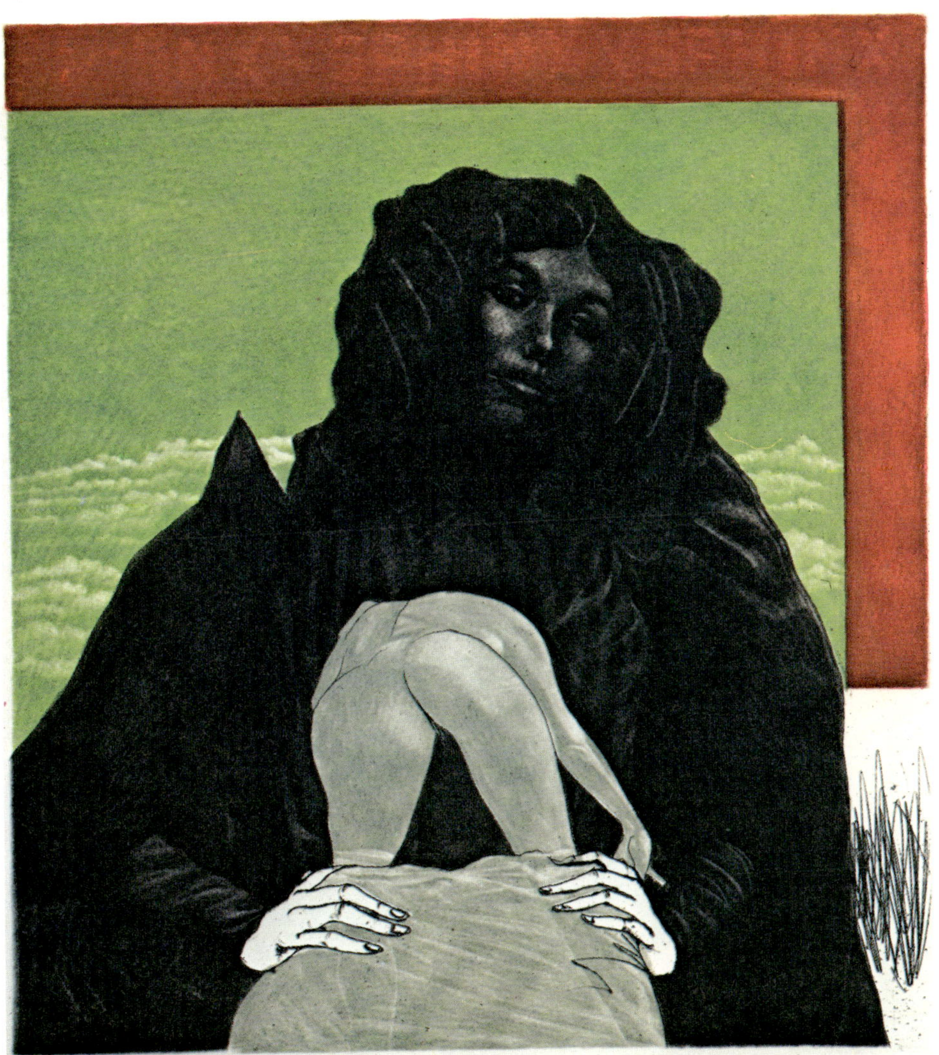

Sphinx in May by Ikeda Masuo
Catalogue number 33

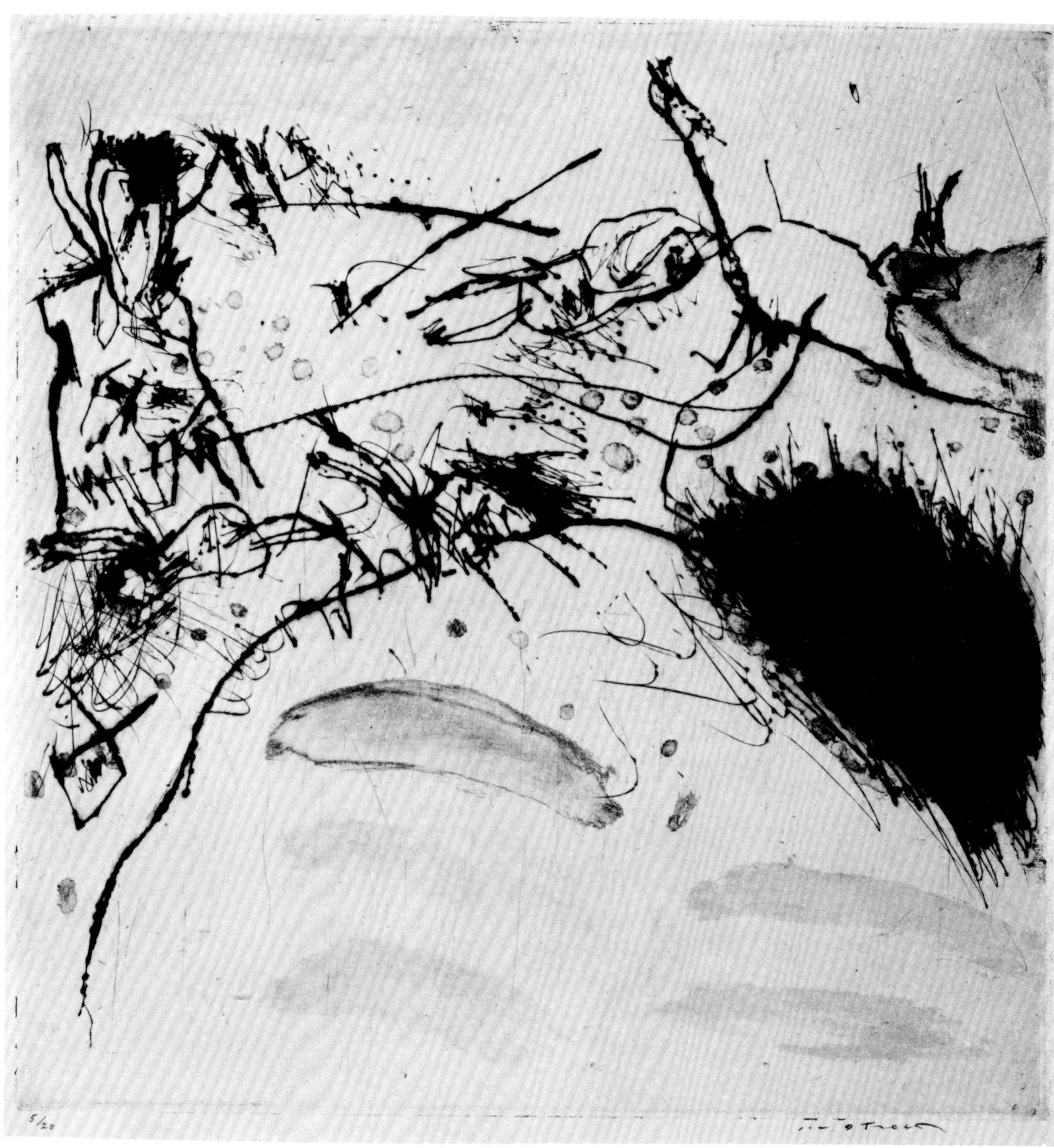

Insect Crossing the Garden by Ikeda Masuo
Catalogue number 6

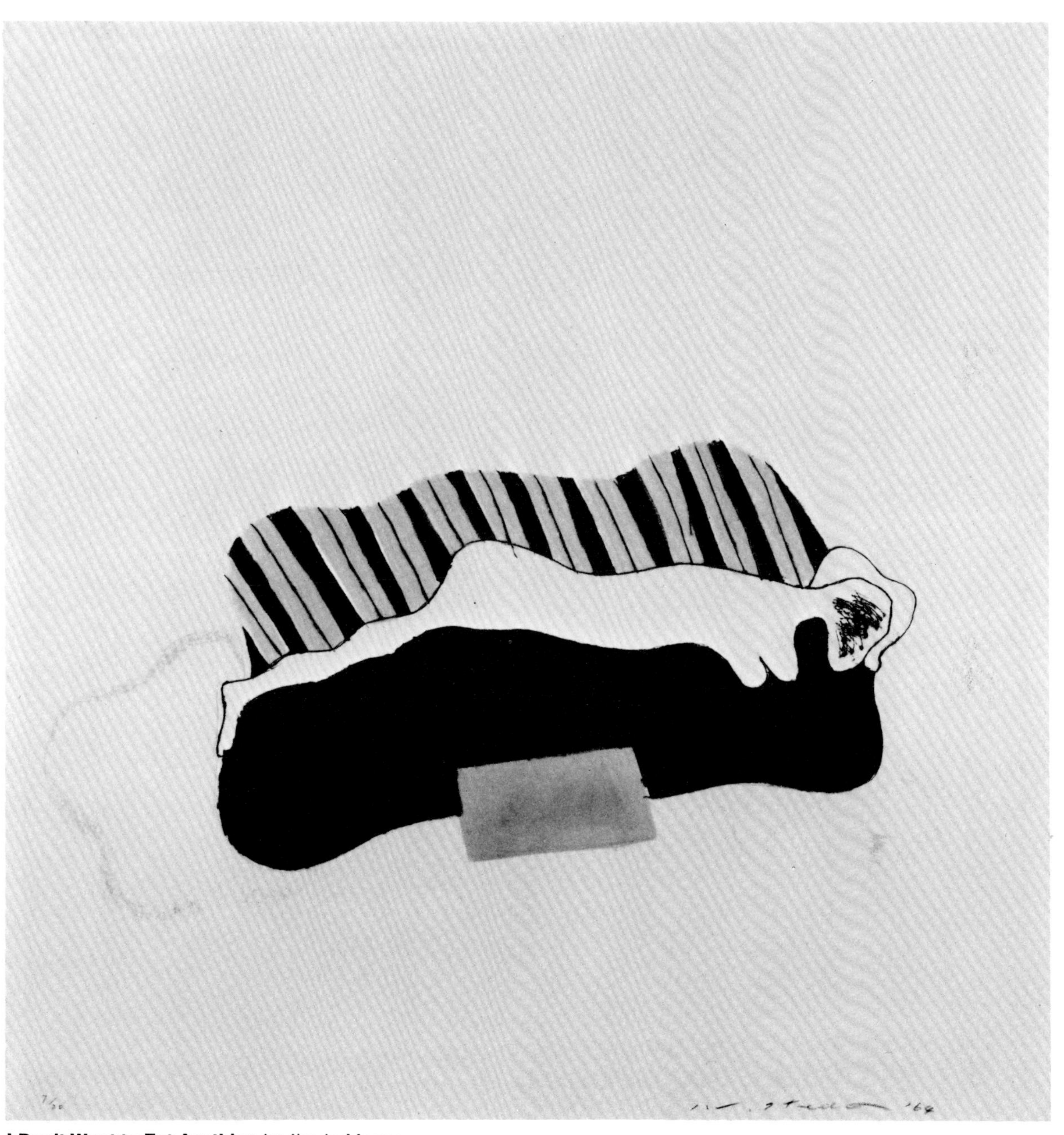

I Don't Want to Eat Anything by Ikeda Masuo
Catalogue number 13

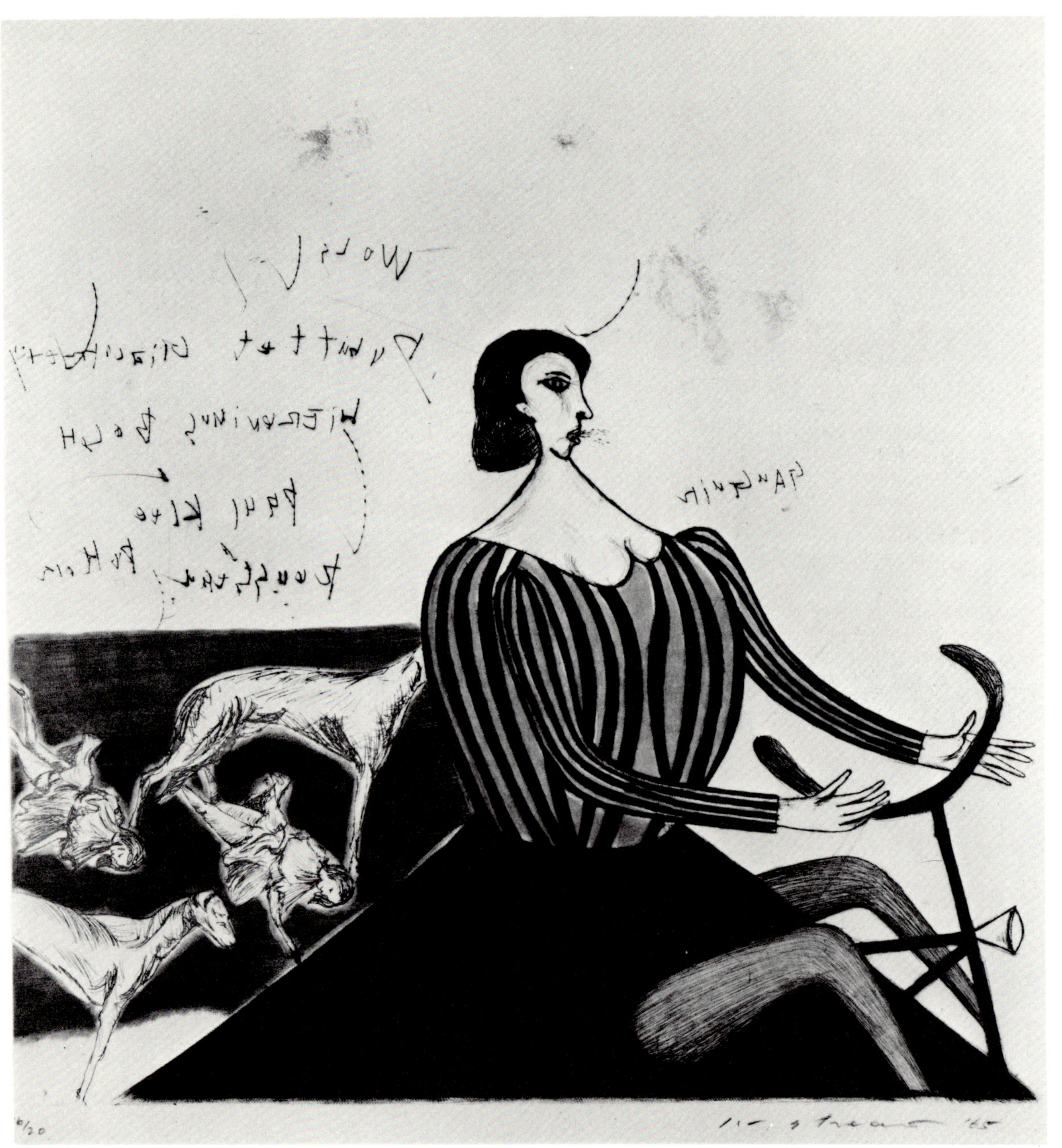

Romantic Scene by Ikeda Masuo
Catalogue number 20

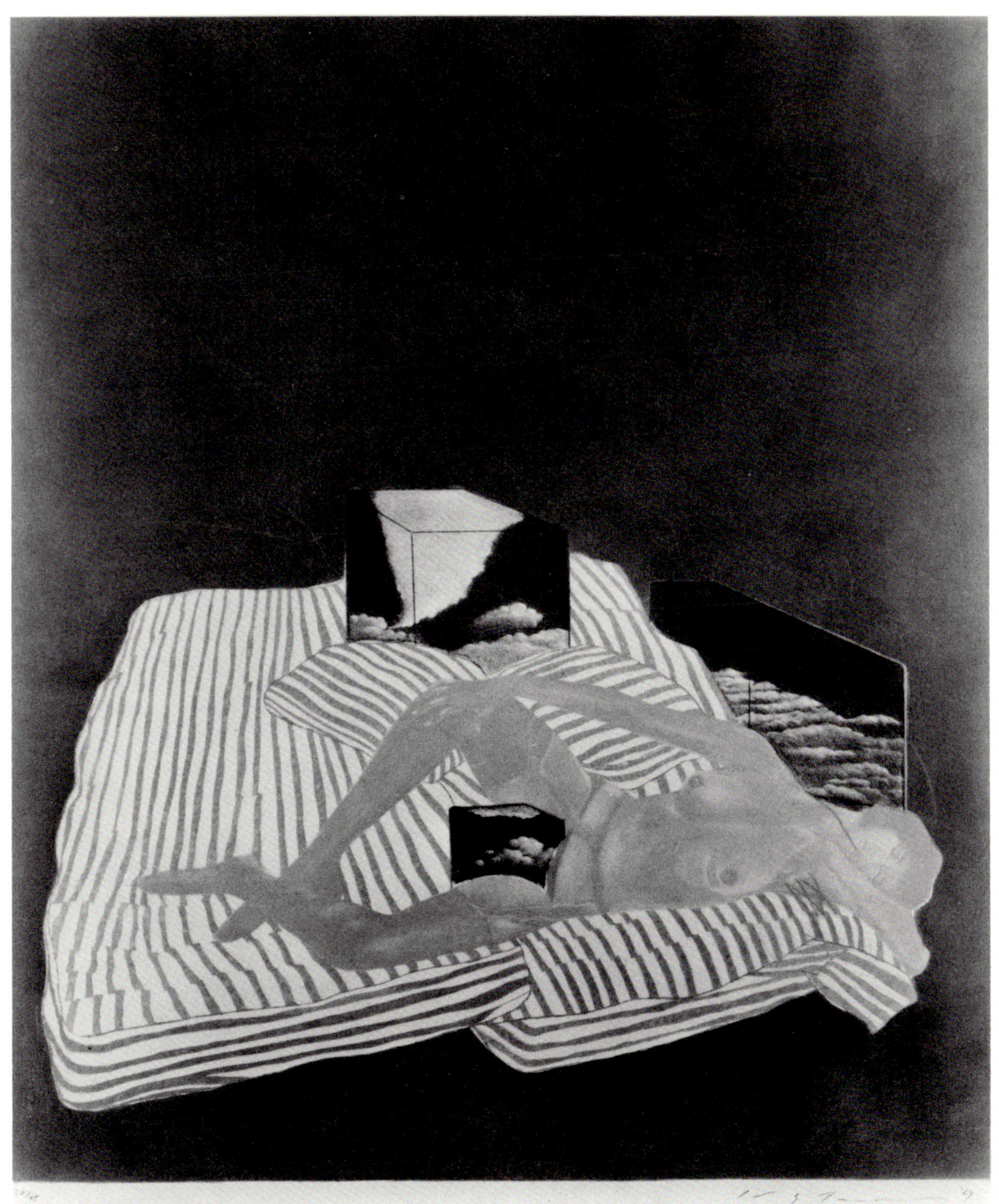

I Continue Sleeping, A by Ikeda Masuo
Catalogue number 27

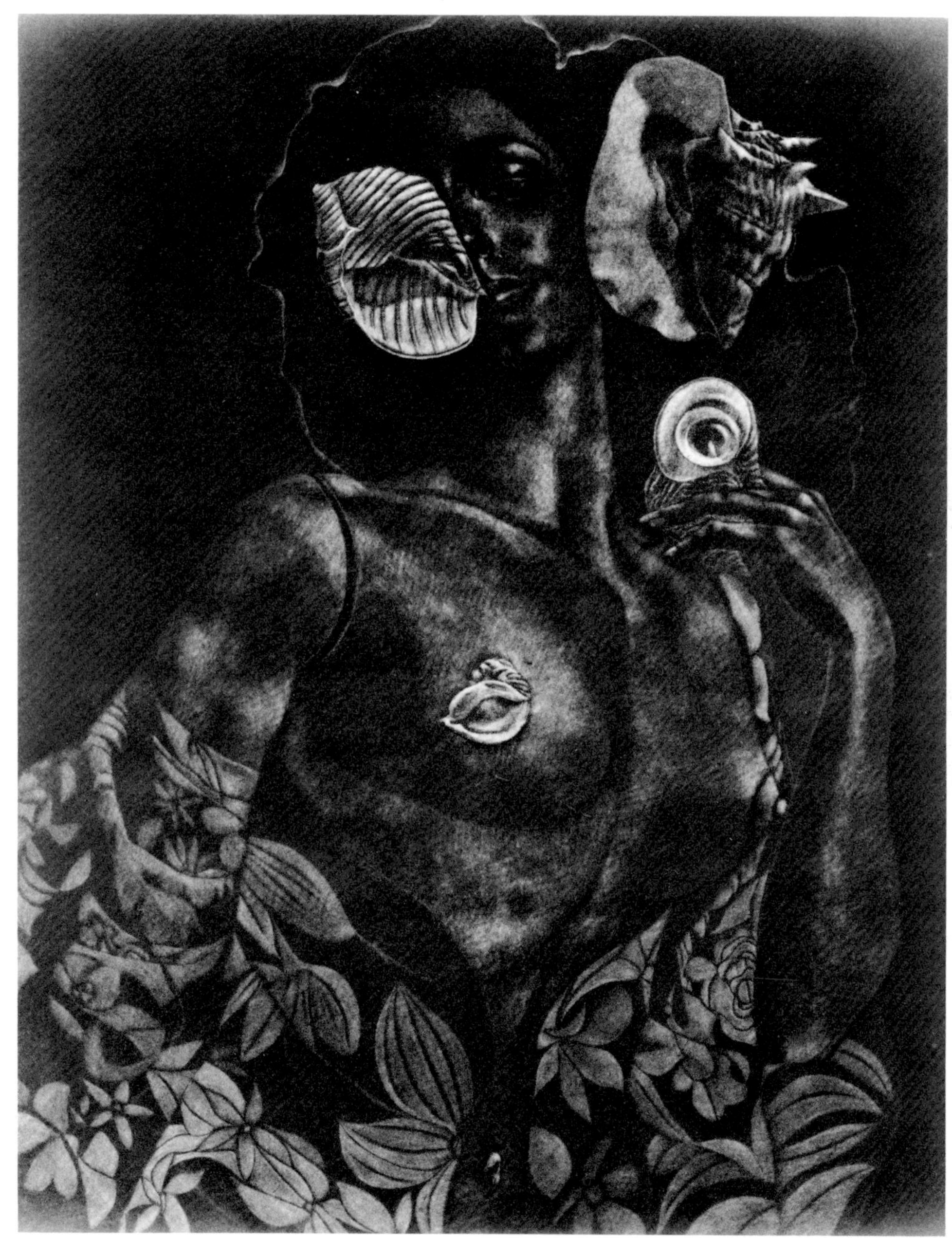

Venus, II by Ikeda Masuo
Catalogue number 40

Catalogue of the Exhibition
Ikeda Masuo

1. Family
1956, Monochrome
Woodcut
5⁹⁄₁₆ x 3¹¹⁄₁₆ inches (14.2 x 9.5 cm.)
Trial Proof only
Mr. Suzuki Yoshio, Nagoya, Japan

2. Jazz
1957, Monochrome
Etching, Aquatint
6½ x 4¾ inches (16.5 x 12 cm.)
Edition 15
Mr. Suzuki Yoshio, Nagoya, Japan

3. L'homme et La Femme, Portfolio
11 sheets
1960
Etching, Hand Colored
4 x 2½ inches (10.2 x 6.4 cm.)
Edition 40, Artist's Proof 10
Mr. Suzuki Yoshio, Nagoya, Japan

4. Woman Animals
1960, Color
Dry Point, Aquatint
9¼ x 7¹⁄₁₆ inches (23.5 x 18 cm.)
Edition 20, Artist's Proof 10
Mr. Suzuki Yoshio, Nagoya, Japan

5. Little More Little Space
1961, Color
Dry Point, Roulette
7¹¹⁄₁₆ x 6¹⁵⁄₁₆ inches (19.5 x 17.5 cm.)
Edition 20
Daisy Viertel Shapiro, New York

6. Insect Crossing the Garden
1962, Color
Dry Point, Etching
14½ x 13¼ inches (36.2 x 33.7 cm.)
Edition 20
The Museum of Modern Art, New York;
Gift of The Felix and Helen Juda
Foundation Illustrated

7. Snake Shaped S
1962, Color
Dry Point, Etching
10⅜ x 7¼ inches (26.3 x 18.5 cm.)
Edition 20
Reiko Ehrman, New York

8. It Rains on Friday
1962, Color
Dry Point, Roulette
14¼ x 14⅛ inches (36.3 x 36 cm.)
Edition 20
Mr. Suzuki Yoshio, Nagoya, Japan

9. Ladies Going to the Door in a Hurry
1963, Color
Dry Point, Roulette
14¹⁄₁₆ x 13⅜ inches (35.7 x 34 cm.)
Edition 20
Mr. Suzuki Yoshio, Nagoya, Japan

10. Taeko's Breakfast
1963, Color
Dry Point, Roulette, Etching
14⅜ x 14 inches (36.5 x 35.5 cm.)
Edition 20
Mr. Suzuki Yoshio, Nagoya, Japan

11. Me Staring at Myself
1964, Color
Dry Point, Roulette, Etching
7⅞ x 7 inches (20 x 17.8 cm.)
Edition 20
The Museum of Modern Art, New York;
Gift of The Felix and Helen Juda Foundation

12. Lady at Her Make-Up
1964, Color
Dry Point, Roulette, Etching
14¼ x 13¼ inches (36.2 x 33.6 cm.)
Edition 20
The Museum of Modern Art, New York;
Gift of The Felix and Helen Juda Foundation

13. I Don't Want to Eat Anything
1964, Color
Dry Point, Roulette, Etching
14⅜ x 13⁹⁄₁₆ inches (36.5 x 34.5 cm.)
Edition 20
Mr. and Mrs. Gordon B. Washburn
Illustrated

14. Miss Rain
1964, Color
Dry Point, Roulette
10¹⁄₁₆ x 9⅝ inches (25.5 x 24.5 cm.)
Edition 20
Miss Alexandra N. Lunn, Washington, D.C.

15. Mari's Chocolate
1964, Color
Dry Point, Roulette
6⅞ x 6⅜ inches (17.8 x 16.3 cm.)
Edition 20
Mr. Emile Dubrule, New York

16. **Charming Soprano**
1964, Color
Dry Point, Roulette, Etching
14⅜ x 13⁹⁄₁₆ inches (36.5 x 34.5 cm.)
Edition 20
Mr. and Mrs. Assa Drori, Los Angeles

17. **Yellow Face**
1965, Color
Dry Point, Roulette, Etching
15¾ x 14⅜ inches (40 x 36.5 cm.)
Edition 20
Mr. and Mrs. Harry H. Lunn, Jr., Washington, D.C.

18. **Sacred Hands, I**
1965, Color
Dry Point, Roulette
14⅜ x 13⁹⁄₁₆ inches (36.5 x 34.5 cm.)
Edition 20
Mr. and Mrs. Felix Juda, Los Angeles

19. **My Poet, My Cat**
1965, Color
Dry Point, Roulette
14⅜ x 13¾ inches (36.5 x 35 cm.)
Edition 20
Barbara Shaw, New York

20. **Romantic Scene**
1965, Color
Dry Point, Roulette
14³⁄₁₆ x 13⁹⁄₁₆ inches (36 x 34.5 cm.)
Edition 20
Mr. Emile Dubrule, New York
Illustrated

21. **Death in Paradise**
1965, Color
Dry Point, Roulette, Etching
15¾ x 14¼ inches (39.9 x 36.2 cm.)
Edition 30
The Museum of Modern Art, New York;
Gift of The Felix and Helen Juda Foundation

22. **Blue Chair**
1966, Color
Dry Point, Roulette, Etching
18 x 18¹⁵⁄₁₆ inches (45.7 x 40.5 cm.)
Edition 30
The Museum of Modern Art, New York;
Gift of The Felix and Helen Juda Foundation

23. **A Certain Relation**
1966, Color
Dry Point, Roulette, Engraving
17¹⁵⁄₁₆ x 16⅛ inches (45.5 x 41 cm.)
Edition 30
Mr. and Mrs. Assa Drori, Los Angeles

24. **Woman from New York**
1966, Color
Lithograph
27⅞ x 21 inches (70.7 x 53.3 cm.)
Edition 20, Tamarind Impressions 9
The Museum of Modern Art, New York;
Gift of Kleiner, Bell and Company

25. **Landscape from Window, A**
1966, Color
Lithograph
28⅞ x 20¾ inches (73.6 x 52.7 cm.)
Edition 20, Tamarind Impressions 9
The Museum of Modern Art, New York;
Gift of Kleiner, Bell and Company

26. **Yellow Sky**
1969, Color
Etching, Roulette, Dry Point, Mezzotint
16¹⁵⁄₁₆ x 14⅛ inches (43 x 36 cm.)
Edition 36
Irene Drori Graphics, Los Angeles

27. **I Continue Sleeping, A**
1969, Color
Etching, Roulette, Dry Point, Mezzotint
27⅜ x 19½ inches (69.5 x 49.5 cm.)
Edition 45
Mr. and Mrs. Yale Kneeland, III, New York
Illustrated

28. **After Dinner, A**
1969, Color
Lithograph
26 x 21¹⁄₁₆ inches (66 x 53.5 cm.)
Edition 100
From the portfolio: "Some Town Without a Name"
Dr. and Mrs. Warren I. Pollock, Wilmington, Delaware

29. **Sphinx of the Woods**
1970, Color
Etching, Roulette, Mezzotint
11⅝ x 10¼ inches (29.5 x 26 cm.)
Edition 60, Special Edition 6
From the portfolio: "Portrait of Sphinx"
The Brooklyn Museum;
Gift of The Felix and Helen Juda Foundation

30. **Sphinx with Little Longer Finger**
1970, Color
Etching, Roulette, Mezzotint
11⅝ x 10¼ inches (29.5 x 26 cm.)
Edition 60, Special Edition 6
From the portfolio: "Portrait of Sphinx"
The Brooklyn Museum;
Gift of The Felix and Helen Juda Foundation

31. Sphinx with the September
1970, Color
Etching, Roulette, Mezzotint
11⅝ x 10¼ inches (29.5 x 26 cm.)
Edition 60, Special Edition 6
From the portfolio: "Portrait of Sphinx"
The Brooklyn Museum;
Gift of The Felix and Helen Juda Foundation

32. Seated Sphinx
1970, Color
Etching, Roulette, Mezzotint
11⅝ x 10¼ inches (29.5 x 26 cm.)
Edition 60, Special Edition 6
From the portfolio: "Portrait of Sphinx"
The Brooklyn Museum;
Gift of The Felix and Helen Juda Foundation

33. Sphinx in May
1970, Color
Etching, Roulette, Mezzotint
11⅝ x 10¼ inches (29.5 x 26 cm.)
Edition 60, Special Edition 6
From the portfolio: "Portrait of Sphinx"
The Brooklyn Museum;
Gift of The Felix and Helen Juda Foundation
Illustrated in Color

34. Sphinx Covered by Sheet
1970, Color
Etching, Roulette, Mezzotint
11⅝ x 10¼ inches (29.5 x 26 cm.)
Edition 60, Special Edition 6
From the portfolio: "Portrait of Sphinx"
The Brooklyn Museum;
Gift of The Felix and Helen Juda Foundation

35. Sphinx of the Woods
1970
2 cancelled copper plates
12 x 10½ inches (30.5 x 26.7 cm.)
The Brooklyn Museum;
Gift of The Felix and Helen Juda Foundation

36. The Seven Deadly Sins
1973, Color
Mezzotint, Dry Point, Etching
11½ x 10¼ inches (29.2 x 26 cm.)
Edition 60, Artist's Proof 20, Special Edition 8
From the portfolio: "The Seven Deadly Sins"
Mr. and Mrs. Yale Kneeland, III, New York

37. Lust
1973, Color
Mezzotint, Dry Point, Etching
11½ x 10¼ inches (29.2 x 26 cm.)
Edition 60, Artist's Proof 20, Special Edition 8
From the portfolio: "The Seven Deadly Sins"
Mr. and Mrs. Yale Kneeland, III, New York

38. Gluttony
1973, Color
Mezzotint, Dry Point, Etching
11½ x 10¼ inches (29.2 x 26 cm.)
Edition 60, Artist's Proof 20, Special Edition 8
From the portfolio: "The Seven Deadly Sins"
Mr. and Mrs. Yale Kneeland, III, New York

39. Venus, I
1974, Color
Mezzotint, Dry Point, Etching
11¾ x 15¾ inches (29.8 x 40 cm.)
Edition 80, Artist's Proof 20, Special Edition 8
From the portfolio: "Venus"
Lent by the Artist

40. Venus, II
1974, Color
Mezzotint, Dry Point, Etching
15¾ x 11¾ inches (40 x 29.8 cm.)
Edition 80, Artist's Proof 20, Special Edition 8
From the portfolio: "Venus"
Lent by the Artist
Illustrated

41. Venus, III
1974, Color
Mezzotint, Dry Point, Etching
11¾ x 15¾ inches (29.8 x 40 cm.)
Edition 80, Artist's Proof 20, Special Edition 8
From the portfolio: "Venus"
Lent by the Artist

Note: Dimensions refer to size of plate or composition
and are given with height preceding width.

Biography/Ikeda Masuo

1934 Ikeda Masuo was born in Mukuden, Manchuria.

1945 Repatriated from Chanchako to Nagano at end of the war.

1952 Moved to Tokyo.

1956 First one-man show of his paintings at the Form Gallery, Tokyo.

Started etching as suggested by Ei-Kyu.

1957 Exhibited at Tokyo International Print Biennial—also in 1960, 1962, 1964, 1966, 1968 and 1970.

1960 First one-man show of his etchings at the Shinobazu Gallery, Tokyo.

Won the first prize in the 2nd International Tokyo Print Biennial; Dr. Will Grohmann recommended him for the prize.

1961 First one-man show of intaglios, Shinobazu Gallery, Tokyo.

Won a prize at Paris Young Artists Biennial.

1962 Won a prize at the 3rd International Tokyo Print Biennial.

1963 One-man show at Nihonbashi Gallery, Tokyo—also in 1964, 1965, 1967 and 1968.

1964 One-man show at Nagoya Form Gallery, Nagoya—also in 1965, 1966 and 1968.

Won National Grand Prize at 4th Tokyo International Print Biennial.

Participated in Contemporary Japanese Art Exhibition, Mainichi Shimbun, Tokyo—also in 1966, 1968, 1969 and 1971.

1965 One-man exhibition at The Museum of Modern Art, New York organized by Mr. William S. Lieberman.

Went to New York for the first time.

One-man show at Associated American Artists, New York—also in 1967, 1969 and 1970.

1966 Received Japan Society Fellowship in New York. Travelled in Europe.

Made lithographs for the first time at The Tamarind Lithography Workshop in Los Angeles with a Ford Foundation Grant.

Awarded the International Grand Prize for graphics at 33rd Venice Biennale.

Retrospective Print Exhibition at Shimano Museum of Modern Art, Nagano.

Won a prize at Krakow International Print Biennial.

Won Education Ministry's Art Award in Japan.

1967 The Museum of Modern Art, New York circulated his prints in a travelling exhibition 1967-69.

One-man show at Keio Department Store— also in 1969 and 1972.

Went to Berlin and was awarded a D.A.A.D. Fellowship by Deutscher Akademischer Austauschdienst.

One-man shows at:
International Artists' Club, Vienna
Galerie Im Erker, St. Gallen, Switzerland
International Culture Center, Budapest
Lumley Cazalet Ltd., London
Kleine Gallery, Germany

1968 One-man shows at:
Gallery Springer, Berlin
Modern Art Gallery, Krakow
Galerie Schneider, Munich

Returned to New York and went to work at Collector's Press.

1969 Exhibition of miniature etchings at Keio Department Store and Hankyu Department Store, Tokyo.

Won a prize at the National Academy of Science and Arts, Yugoslavia

Won a prize at 8th Ljubljana International Print Biennial.

One-man shows at:
  Graphic Gallery, San Francisco
  Osaka Form Gallery, Fukuoka

1970 One-man shows at:
  Nantenshi Gallery, Tokyo
  Lunn Gallery, Washington, D.C.
  Bancho Gallery, Tokyo
Won a prize at 3rd Krakow International
Print Biennial.
Won an award at 17th Annual Brooklyn
Museum Print Exhibition.

1971 One-man show at The Brooklyn Museum,
New York.
One-man show at Long Beach Museum of
Art, California.
One-man shows at:
  Umeda Gallery, Osaka
  Bancho Gallery, Tokyo
  Nagoya Gallery, Nagoya
  Nantenshi Gallery, Tokyo

1972 Won a prize at the International Cultureel
Centrum, Antwerpen, Netherlands.
One-man show at the University of Maine.
Moved from New York City to East
Hampton where he still lives.

1973 One-man shows at:
  Prints on Prince Street, New York
  Nantenshi Gallery, Tokyo
  Lunn Gallery, Washington, D.C.

1974 "Ikeda & Ida: Two New Japanese Print-
makers", Japan House Gallery, New York.
Watercolor Exhibition, Staempfli Gallery,
New York.
Collage Exhibition, Bancho Gallery, Tokyo.
"My Imagination Map", Central Museum,
Tokyo.

Public Collections/Ikeda Masuo

Achenbach Foundation, San Francisco
Albertina Museum, Vienna
The Art Institute of Chicago
Baltimore Museum of Art
The Brooklyn Museum
Cincinnati Art Museum
Grunwald Foundation, Los Angeles
Hyogo County Museum
Japan House Gallery, New York
Jerusalem Museum, Israel
Felix and Helen Juda Foundation, Los Angeles
Kamakura Museum of Modern Art
Library of Congress, Washington, D.C.
Los Angeles County Museum of Art
The Metropolitan Museum of Art, New York
The Minneapolis Institute of Arts
Museum of Fine Arts, Boston
The Museum of Modern Art, New York
Museum of Modern Art, Rome
Nagaoka Contemporary Museum
National Museum of Krakow
National Museum of Modern Art, Tokyo
National Museum of Oslo
National Museum of Warsaw
Newark Museum, New Jersey
Philadelphia Museum of Art
San Francisco Museum of Art
Seattle Art Museum

IDA SHOICHI

Ida Shoichi

Ida is probably the more difficult of the two print artists—difficult in the sense of getting at his ideas and meanings in prints, for they are filled with allusions and illusions covered over with a distinctly un-Japanese color sense. He veils his very serious purposes with an outrage of pink or baby blue or orange, or sometimes, by an introduction of too familiar—if not banal—patterns that rest disquietingly just above the surface of meaning.

He is a singular artist, uncompromising in his pursuits, unwilling or unable to churn out saleable products, but one who has a fiercely loyal following in Japan and in the United States, and who exhibits where and when he chooses.

He has always lived in Kyoto, and his knowledge of the ancient city, of its lore, art, and people is formidable. More formidable still is his knowledge of the print medium. There is no technique he has not studied and taught. He has elected, however, to work almost exclusively with lithograph and silkscreen, two of the less labored print techniques.

Ida's early prints were of simple forms of intense coloring. "Pink Mama" is one that comes to mind; a stylized bust portrait of a woman whose hair lets down in pink and green. It is an effective, sun-lit impression of voluptuousness.

The 1969 prints produced during his stay in Paris, London, and the United States differ from what came before and what was to follow. Outstanding among these are the rare etchings Ida did in Paris and London, the "Shoe" series. Evoking a wet London with subtle colors and sharp lines the example in the exhibition is unusually subdued for the artist.

Returning to Japan the artist immediately embarked upon a successful series which showed for the first time his completely unique use of color. From 1967 through 1970 Ida continued to develop an identity with harshly bright colors; "Pansy", "Baby", and, finally "Black Sofa" show recognizable objects suspended in lightness. There is a tendency in these to muddy the color, which in turn gives a greater depth to the color but which also has the effect of holding a viewer at bay. This is the first hint in Ida's work of ambivalence towards his audience. This, as it continues in his work, tends to create a tension between viewer and print. He provokes with color as much as with his unpredictability.

In 1971 the artist, then teaching at Kyoto Arts College, started a silkscreen "Grass" series. These prints—"Morning Grass", "Pink Grass", "Tissue on the Grass"

—are among his most accomplished to date. Here the complete sheet is printed with a perfect balance of object and color. The elements are most successfully disposed. The tissues, crumpled, on wet or windblown grasses and deliberately obscured by photographic and printing techniques, are most like the *kaishi* napkins familiar in *kabuki* and tea ceremony but here having a pronounced erotic *ukiyo-e* effect.

In 1972 the artist continued in his use of strong color and subtle subject. His "Shade of Tree", perhaps the most revealing of all Ida's prints to date, is simply beautiful—in design, execution, color, and subject this print in its several variations reveals a sentiment which is traditionally Japanese: a celebration of nature, but not a nature without man or at odds with man. The leaves that are so elegantly disposed on the surface are surely the product of a Japanese gardener's hand. They relate here closely to Sakai Hoitsu and the Rimpa artists. It is a rare case in which the artist—just for the love of it—plainly reveals himself as a person, as a Japanese.

At the same time Ida produced "Measure and Pig", "Flags of Blue", and "Well! Morning", the last a romantic portrait of an old black telephone.

In the following year—working at a feverish pace—the artist began to introduce foreign elements into (onto) his prints. String, penny balloons, printed polyester film, and importantly, rubber foam or sponge were added.

For Ida this had enormous consequences. His respect for paper is greater than that I have seen in any other artist. He had thoroughly researched Japanese paper and used only the finest quality hand-made *washi.* Purchased from the craftsman at considerable cost, he seemed to have an almost Shinto attitude towards the "purity" and "sanctity" of the individual sheet. (There are scholars in Japan who believe the craft of folding paper, *origami,* began because of the potential "divinity" of individual sheets, not to be destroyed by cutting, and this from the influence of Shinto teachings.)

The effect upon the artist was liberating. His introduction of printed foam rubber into his 1973 prints made a significant change in his surface. These especially, "Pig Wall" and "Lucy in the Sky" manifest entirely new possibilities in print art.

With much heralded shows in Osaka, Kyoto, and Tokyo this year Ida seems to be coming into his own. He is a radical printmaker, not especially interested in being understood, but richly rewarding to anyone who wants to try.

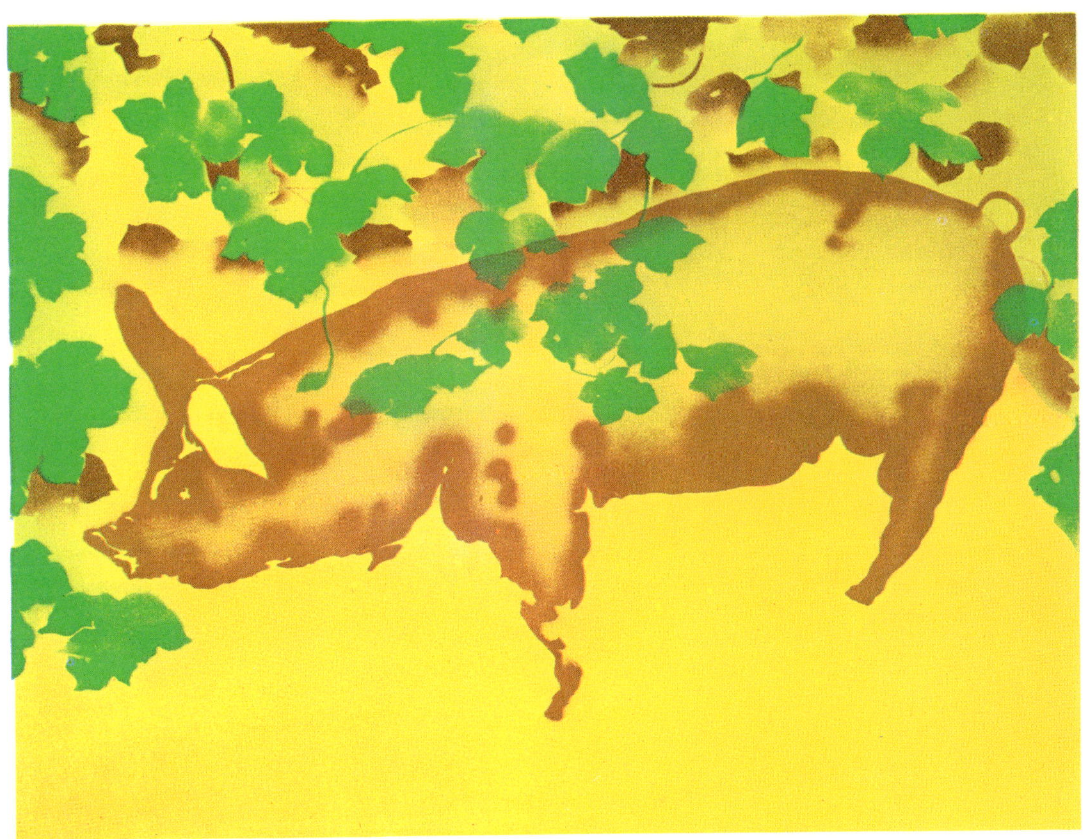

Shade of a Tree by Ida Shoichi
Catalogue number 16

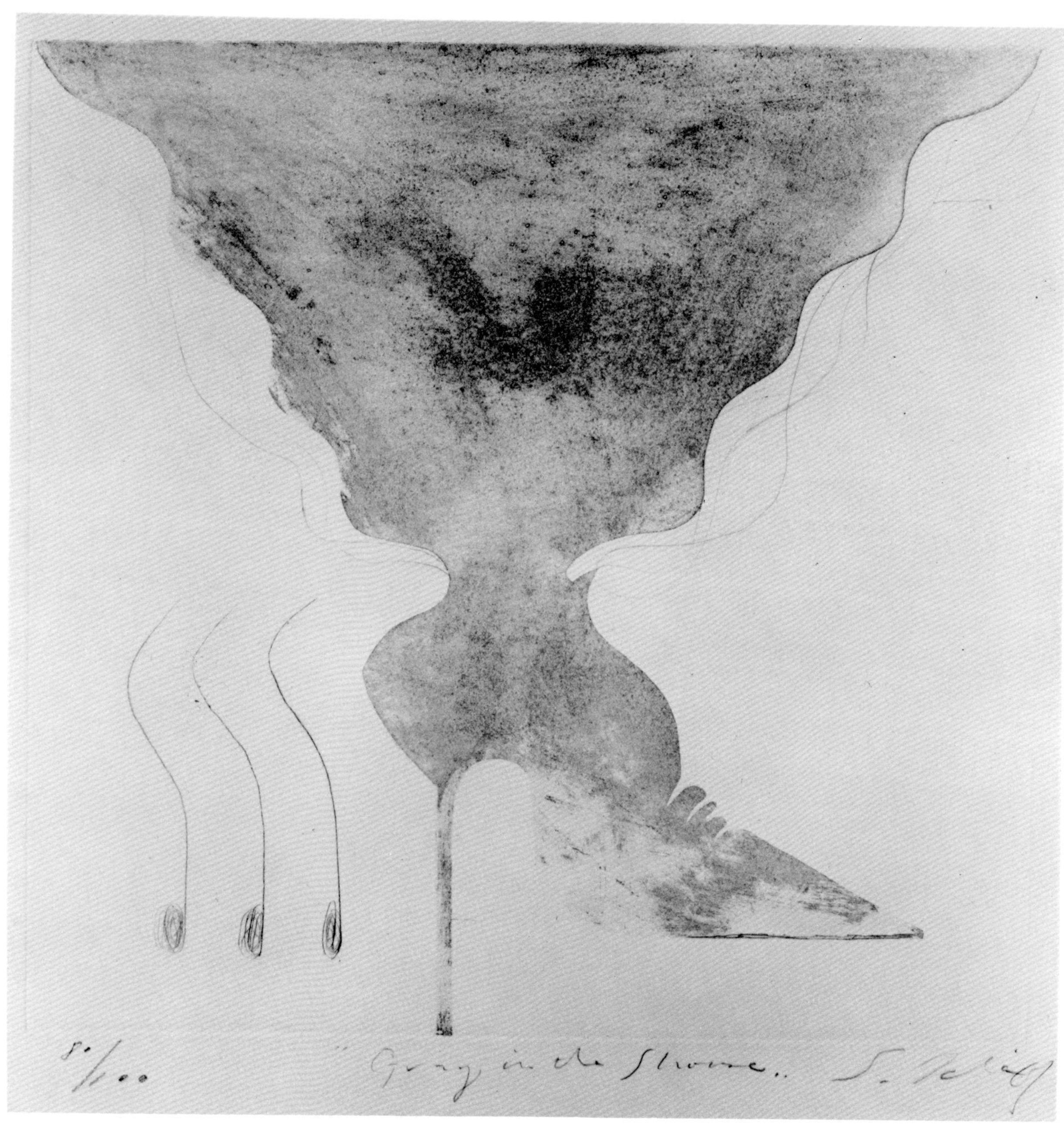

Grey in the Shoe by Ida Shoichi
Catalogue number 3

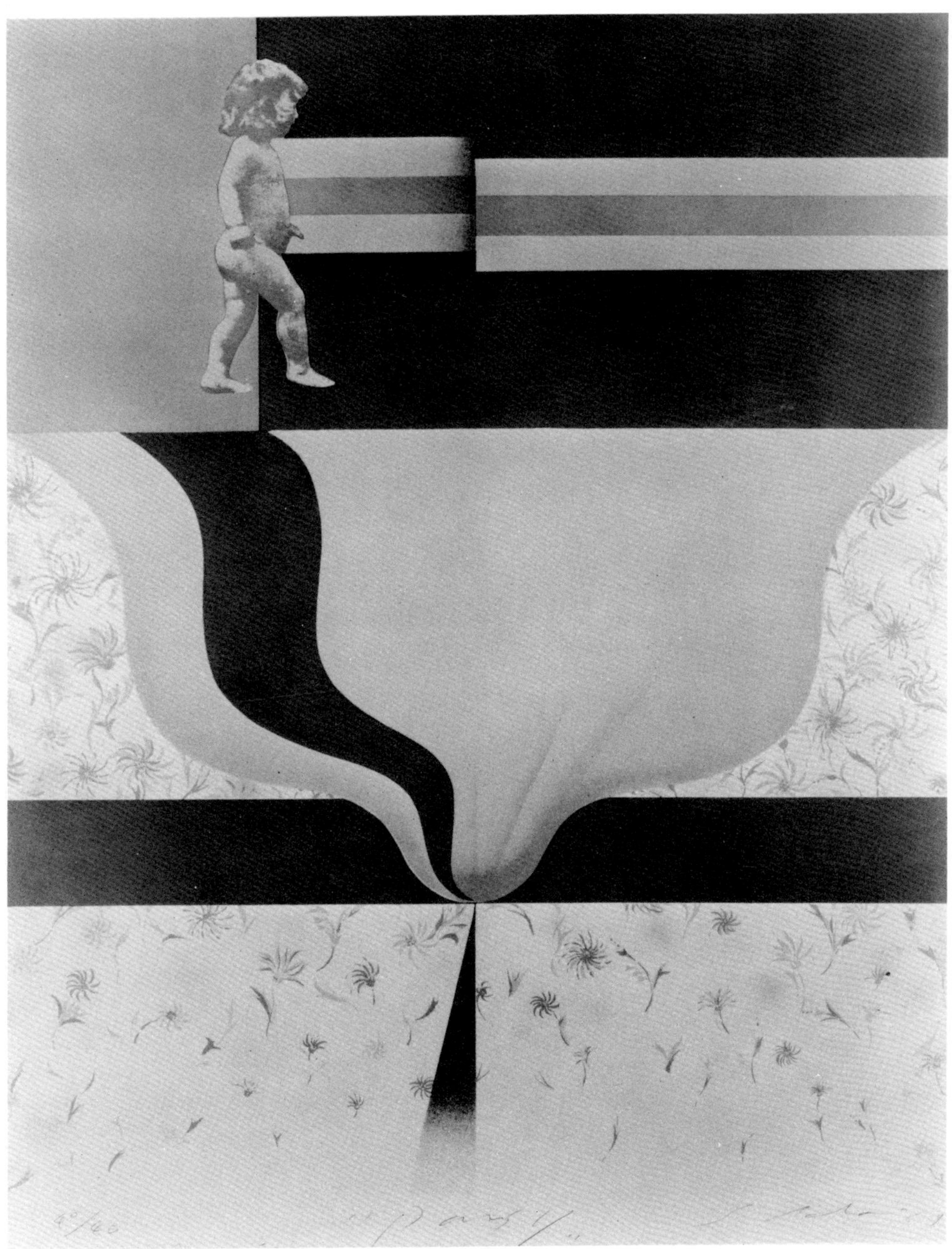

Pansy by Ida Shoichi
Catalogue number 4

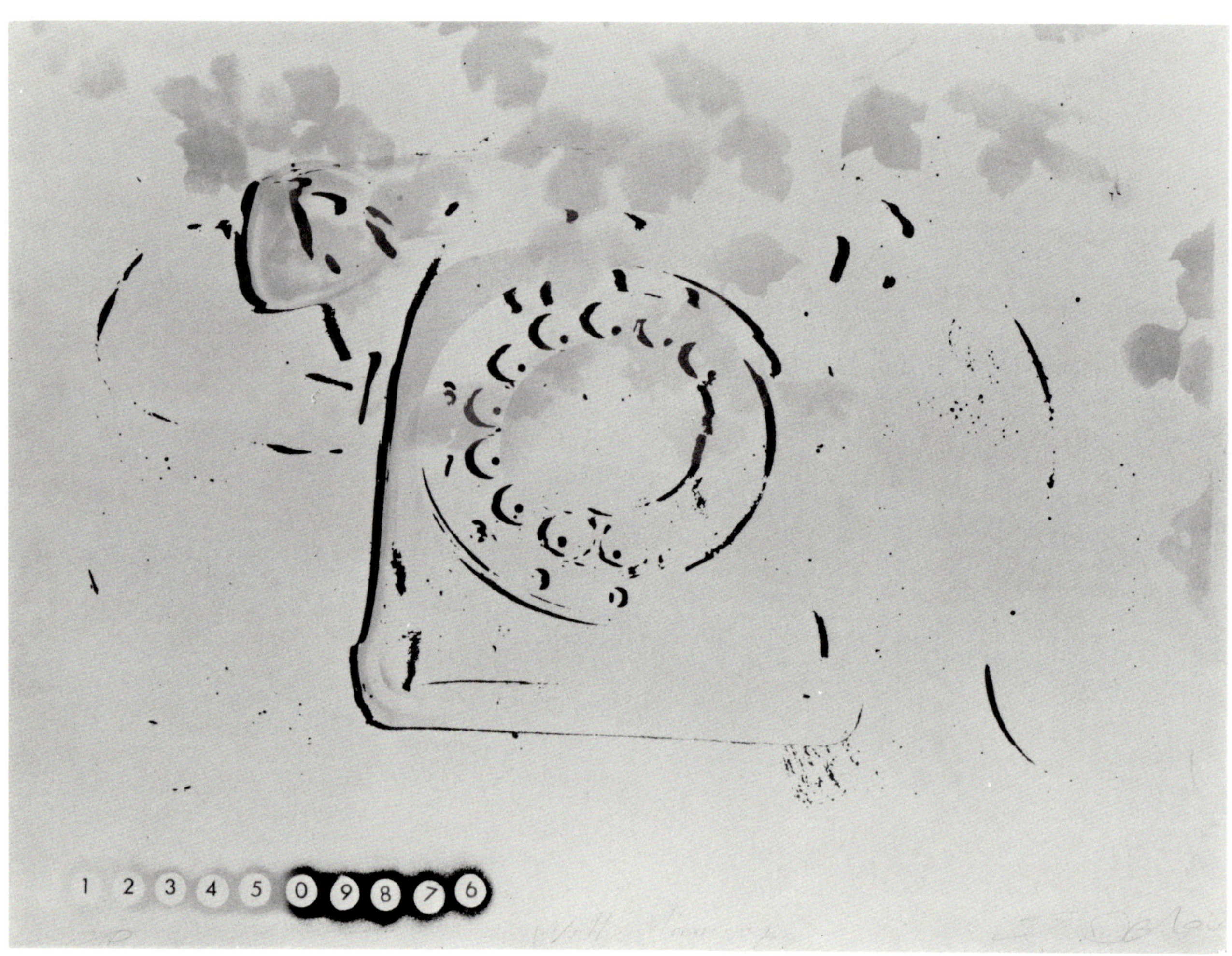

Well! Morning by Ida Shoichi
Catalogue number 20

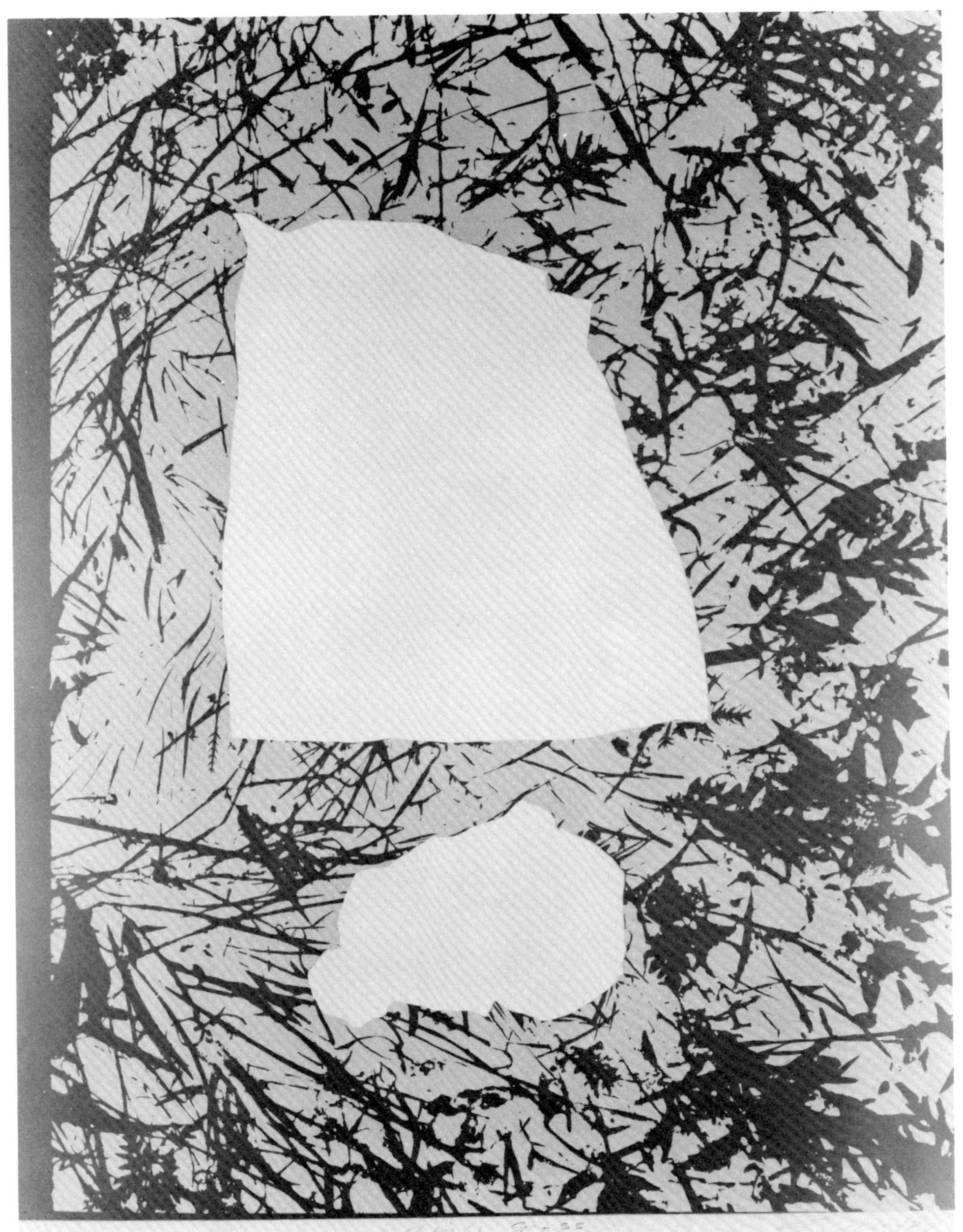

Pink Grass by Ida Shoichi
Catalogue number 9

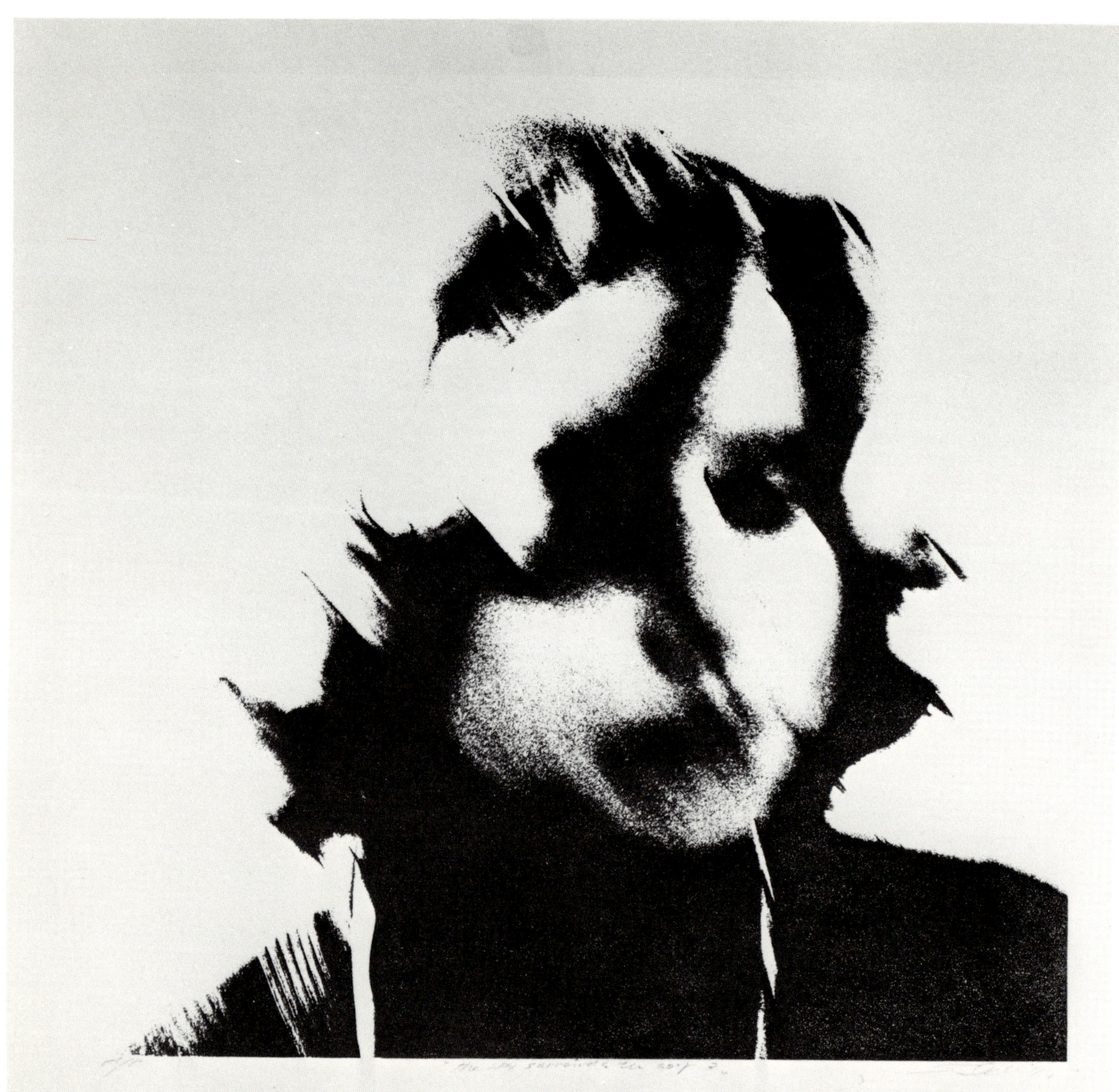

The Spy Surrounds the Spy 3 by Ida Soichi
Catalogue number 35

Catalogue of the Exhibition
Ida Shoichi

1. Heart 1, Heart 2, Diptych
1965, Color
Lithograph on *Daishowa* paper
9¹/₁₆ x 21¼ inches (23 x 54 cm.)
Edition 30, Artist's Proof 3
Connie Kimos, Kyoto, Japan

2. Pink Mama
1966, Color
Lithograph on *Fukuishi* paper
26 x 20⅝ inches (66 x 52.5 cm.)
Edition 10, Artist's Proof 2
Mr. and Mrs. Yale Kneeland, III, New York

3. Grey in the Shoe
1969-70, Color
Dry Point, Aquatint on B.F.K. paper
11½ x 11½ inches (29.2 x 29.2 cm.)
Edition 100, Artist's Proof 10
From the series: "Rain"
Anonymous
Illustrated

4. Pansy, Triptych
1969, Color
Lithograph, Photo-silkscreen on *Fukuishi* paper
27⅝ x 21⅜ inches (70.2 x 54.3 cm.)
Edition 40, Artist's Proof 5
From the series: "Pansy"
Horie Yasuko, Sakai, Japan
One part triptych illustrated

5. Baby
1970, Color
Lithograph, Photo-silkscreen on *Fukuishi* paper
22⅜ x 27³/₁₆ inches (56.8 x 69 cm.)
Edition 75, Artist's Proof 3
Shibatani Coco, Kyoto, Japan

6. Pink of Place
1970, Color
Lithograph on *Daishowa* paper
25³/₁₆ x 20½ inches (64 x 52 cm.)
Edition 30, Artist's Proof 3
The National Museum of Modern Art, Kyoto, Japan

7. Black Sofa
1970, Color
Lithograph on *Daishowa* paper
25 x 20⁷/₁₆ inches (63.5 x 51.9 cm.)
Edition 30, Artist's Proof 3
The Museum of Modern Art, New York;
Gift of Mr. and Mrs. Wolfgang Schoenborn

8. Morning Grass
1971, Color
Photo-silkscreen on *Daishowa* paper
21⅜ x 27⅝ inches (54.3 x 70.1 cm.)
Edition 75, Artist's Proof 8
From the series: "Tissues"
Lent by the Artist

9. Pink Grass
1971, Color
Photo-silkscreen on *Daishowa* paper
28¹⁵/₁₆ x 21⅜ inches (73.5 x 54.3 cm.)
Edition 75, Artist's Proof 8
From the series: "Tissue"
Lent by the Artist
Illustrated

10. Five Mamas
1971, Color
Photo-silkscreen on *Daishowa* paper
28½ x 21⅛ inches (72.4 x 53.6 cm.)
Edition 75, Artist's Proof 8
From the series: "Tissue"
Anonymous

11. Tissue on the Grass
1971, Color
Photo-silkscreen on *Daishowa* paper
21⅜ x 27⅛ inches (54.3 x 68.9 cm.)
Edition 75, Artist's Proof 8
From the series: "Tissue"
Lent by the Artist

12. Dance on the Grass
1971, Color
Photo-silkscreen on *Daishowa* paper
29¾ x 21⅛ inches (75.6 x 53.6 cm.)
Edition 75, Artist's Proof 8
From the series: "Tissue"
Anonymous

13. White Tissue
1971, Color
Photo-silkscreen on *Daishowa* paper
28½ x 21⅜ inches (72.4 x 54.3 cm.)
Edition 75, Artist's Proof 8
From the series: "Tissue"
Lent by the Artist

14. Romance
1971, Color
Photo-silkscreen on *Daishowa* paper
29¾ x 21⅛ inches (75.6 x 53.6 cm.)
Edition 75, Artist's Proof 8
From the series: "Tissue"
Lent by the Artist

15. **Long Paper**
1972, Color
Lithograph (zinc plate) on M.O. paper
21⅞ x 28¼ inches (55.5 x 71.7 cm.)
Edition 30, Artist's Proof 3
Mr. and Mrs. Yale Kneeland, III, New York

16. **Shade of a Tree**
1972, Color
Lithograph (zinc plate) on M.O. paper
22¼ x 28⅛ inches (56.5 x 71.5 cm.)
Edition 30, Artist's Proof 3
Mr. and Mrs. Yale Kneeland, III, New York
Illustrated in Color

17. **Measure and Pig**
1972, Color
Lithograph (zinc plate and stone) on M.O. paper
22 1/16 x 29⅛ inches (56 x 74 cm.)
Edition 30, Artist's Proof 3
Mr. and Mrs. Yale Kneeland, III, New York

18. **Gray Scale,** Diptych
1972, Color
Lithograph (zinc and aluminum plate) on B.F.K. paper
27⅝ x 21¼ inches (70.2 x 54 cm.) each
Edition 30, Artist's Proof 3
From the series: "Pink of Place"
Mr. Kurusina Barunie, Tokyo, Japan

19. **Flags of Blue**
1972, Color
Lithograph, Etching on M.O. paper
21⅞ x 27⅞ inches (55.5 x 70.9 cm.)
Edition 30, Artist's Proof 3
Mr. and Mrs. Yale Kneeland, III, New York

20. **Well! Morning**
1972, Color
Lithograph (zinc plate) on White Crisbrook paper
22⅛ x 28⅞ inches (56.2 x 73.5 cm.)
Edition 30, Artist's Proof 5
Mr. and Mrs. G. Peabody Gardner, III, New York
Illustrated

21. **Wallpaper Pig—1**
1973, Color
Lithograph (zinc plate) on *Hanga* paper
21¼ x 27 9/16 inches (54 x 70 cm.)
Edition 30, Artist's Proof 3
From the series: "La Vie en Rose"
Lent by the Artist

22. **Wallpaper Pig—4**
1973, Color
Lithograph (zinc plate) on *Hanga* paper
21¼ x 27¾ inches (54 x 70.5 cm.)
Edition 30, Artist's Proof 3
From the series: "La Vie en Rose"
Anonymous

23. **Pig Wall**
1973, Color
Lithograph on *Hanga* paper; silkscreen on foam rubber
21½ x 27 9/16 x ¾ inches (54.6 x 70 x 2 cm.)
Edition 30, Artist's Proof 3
From the series: "La Vie en Rose"
Mr. and Mrs. Yale Kneeland, III, New York

24. **Sprayed Helicopter No. 2**
1973, Color
Lithograph with punched eyelet and yarn on *Hanga* paper
22¼ x 28⅛ inches (56.5 x 71.5 cm.)
Edition 30, Artist's Proof 3
From the series: "Wind and La Vie en Rose"
Mr. and Mrs. Yale Kneeland, III, New York

25. **Sprayed Dogs**
1973, Color
Lithograph on *Hanga* paper with polyester film and
punched eyelet
21¼ x 27¾ inches (54 x 70.5 cm.)
Edition 30, Artist's Proof 3
Maekawa Mitsuko, New York

26. **Sprayed Rose**
1973, Color
Lithograph on black plastic paper and polyester film
with rope and ring
21¼ x 27¾ inches (54 x 70.5 cm.)
Edition 30, Artist's Proof 3
From the series: "Wind and La Vie en Rose"
Himeji Gallery, Tokyo, Japan

27. **Stop the Rain**
1973, Color
Lithograph (zinc plate) on *Hanga* paper
27 15/16 x 21 7/16 inches (71 x 54.5 cm.)
Edition 30, Artist's Proof 3
From the series: "Wind and La Vie en Rose"
Anonymous

28. **Wind into the Woods**
1973, Color
Lithograph (zinc plate) on *Hanga* paper and polyester
film with punched eyelet
27 15/16 x 21 7/16 inches (71 x 54.5 cm.)
Edition 30, Artist's Proof 3
From the series: "Wind and La Vie en Rose"
Lent by the Artist

29. **Wind Dance**
   1973, Color
   Lithograph (zinc plate) on *Hanga* paper
   28⅜ x 22⅛ inches (72 x 56.2 cm.)
   Edition 30, Artist's Proof 3
   From the series: "Wind and La Vie en Rose"
   Mr. and Mrs. Yale Kneeland, III, New York

30. **Orange Sister**
   8 sheets of 140 unsigned wall paper sheets
   1973, Color
   Offset (aluminum plate) on *Joshitsu* paper
   29½ x 22½ inches (75 x 57.1 cm.)
   Edition 30, Artist's Proof 3
   Lent by the Artist

31. **Letter**
   1974, Color
   Lithograph (zinc plate and stone), silkscreen on white
   Crisbrook paper
   26⁹⁄₁₆ x 21¹⁄₁₆ inches (67.5 x 53.5 cm.)
   Edition 30, Artist's Proof 3
   From the series: "The Spy Surrounds the Spy"
   Lent by the Artist

32. **Black Letter**
   1974, Color
   Lithograph (zinc plate and stone) on *Kozo, Mitsumata*
   and *Torinoko* paper
   17¾ x 17¾ inches (45 x 45 cm.)
   Edition 30, Artist's Proof 3
   From the series: "The Spy Surrounds the Spy"
   Lent by the Artist

33. **The Spy Surrounds the Spy 1**
   1974, Color
   Lithograph (zinc plate and stone) on *Kozo, Mitsumata*
   and *Torinoko* paper
   17¾ x 17¾ inches (45 x 45 cm.)
   Edition 20, Artist's Proof 2
   From a portfolio of 100 prints
   Lent by the Artist

34. **The Spy Surrounds the Spy 2**
   1974, Color
   Lithograph (zinc plate and stone) on *Kozo, Mitsumata*
   and *Torinoko* paper
   17¾ x 17¾ inches (45 x 45 cm.)
   Edition 20, Artist's Proof 2
   From a portfolio of 100 prints
   Lent by the Artist

35. **The Spy Surrounds the Spy 3**
   1974, Color
   Lithograph (zinc plate and stone) on *Kozo, Mitsumata*
   and *Torinoko* paper
   17¾ x 17¾ inches (45 x 45 cm.)
   Edition 20, Artist's Proof 2
   From a portfolio of 100 prints
   Lent by the Artist
   Illustrated

36. **The Spy Surrounds the Spy 4**
   1974, Color
   Lithograph (zinc plate and stone) on *Kozo, Mitsumata*
   and *Torinoko* paper
   17¾ x 17¾ inches (45 x 45 cm.)
   Edition 20, Artist's Proof 2
   From a portfolio of 100 prints
   Lent by the Artist

37. **The Spy Surrounds the Spy 5**
   1974, Color
   Lithograph (zinc plate and stone) on *Kozo, Mitsumata*
   and *Torinoko* paper
   17¾ x 17¾ inches (45 x 45 cm.)
   Edition 20, Artist's Proof 2
   From a portfolio of 100 prints
   Lent by the Artist

38. **The Spy Surrounds the Spy 6**
   1974, Color
   Lithograph (zinc plate and stone) on *Kozo, Mitsumata*
   and *Torinoko* paper
   17¾ x 17¾ inches (45 x 45 cm.)
   Edition 20, Artist's Proof 2
   From a portfolio of 100 prints
   Lent by the Artist

39. **The Spy Surrounds the Spy 7**
   1974, Color
   Lithograph (zinc plate and stone) on *Kozo, Mitsumata*
   and *Torinoko* paper
   17¾ x 17¾ inches (45 x 45 cm.)
   Edition 20, Artist's Proof 2
   From a portfolio of 100 prints
   Lent by the Artist

40. **The Spy Surrounds the Spy 8**
   1974, Color
   Lithograph (zinc plate and stone) on *Kozo, Mitsumata*
   and *Torinoko* paper
   17¾ x 17¾ inches (45 x 45 cm.)
   Edition 20, Artist's Proof 2
   From a portfolio of 100 prints
   Lent by the Artist

Note: Dimensions refer to size of plate or composition and
are given with height preceding width.

Biography/Ida Shoichi

1940   Ida Shoichi was born in Kyoto, Japan.

1965   Completed the Post Graduate Course of Kyoto Municipal University of Art, Oil Painting Department.

Participated in the 1st Exhibition of Mainichi Art Concours by the French Government at the Kyoto Municipal Museum of Fine Art.

1967   Participated in:
The 2nd Exhibition of Mainichi Art Concours by the French Government at the Kyoto Municipal Museum of Fine Art.

Exhibition of Trend in Contemporary Japanese Art at the National Museum of Modern Art, Kyoto.

1968   Participated in the 3rd Exhibition of Mainichi Art Concours by the French Government at the Kyoto Municipal Museum of Fine Art.

Received an award to go to Paris.

Participated in the 6th International Tokyo Print Biennial.

1969   Travelled to Paris.

Participated in:
The 1st International Biennial Exhibition of Prints, Florence.

Essai de Graphie, Paris.

The International Biennial Exhibition of Young Printers, Vancouver, Canada.

The 9th Contemporary Art Exhibition of Japan, Tokyo City Museum of Fine Art

Exhibition of Contemporary, Japanese Prints of 18 Artists, Kyoto Municipal Museum of Fine Art.

1970   Travelled to New York.
Participated in:
The 7th International Tokyo Print Biennial.

The 2nd Biennale International de l'Estampe, Paris.

The 1st Ausstellung International Exhibition of Graphics and Illustration, Frechen, Germany.

The Frontier of Contemporary Japanese Prints, Sapporo Cultural Center, Sapporo.

Patronat Tremi International Dihuix, Joan Miro, Barcelona, Spain.

The 3rd Krakow International Print Biennial.

The 3rd Salon International de Galeries Pilotes, Musee Cantonal des Beaux-Arts, Lausanne.

1971   Participated in:
The 9th Ljubljana International Print Biennial.

Exhibition of Contemporary Prints of Japan, Brussels.

Exhibition of Contemporary Prints, Mexico City.

The International Biennial of Young Printers, Vancouver, Canada.

The Exhibition "Eyes", New York.

Exhibition of Contemporary Art, Museum of Modern Art, Wakayama.

Exhibition of 100 Artists of Today, Municipal Museum of Modern Art, Hyogo.

1972   Participated in:
The 4th Krakow International Print Biennial.

The 3rd Bradford International Print
Biennial Exhibition, England.

The 2nd Ausstellung International
Exhibition of Graphics, Frechen, Germany.

The 3rd Paris International Biennial
Exhibition of Print.

Exhibition of Contemporary Japanese
Prints, Kentucky.

1973   Participated in:
The 10th Ljubljana International Print
Biennial.

Exhibition of Lithograph Today circulated
by Pratt Graphic Center, New York.

Exhibition of New Prints from Japan,
Pratt Graphic Center, New York.

Exhibition of Contemporary Japanese
Prints, South Africa.

One-man show at Gallery Coco, Kyoto.

One-man show at Shinanobashi Gallery,
Osaka.

1974   One-man show at Himeji Gallery, Tokyo.

Multimedia exhibition at American Center,
Kyoto.

"Ikeda & Ida: Two New Japanese Printmakers", Japan House Gallery, New York.

Public Collections/Ida Shoichi

Belgium Royal Library of Brussels
Helsinki Museum
Japan House Gallery, New York
Kyoto Municipal Museum of Fine Art
The Museum of Modern Art, New York
National Library of Paris
The National Museum of Modern Art, Kyoto
New York Public Library
Paris City Museum of Modern Art
Stedelyc Museum, Amsterdam
Victoria Albert Museum, London

Friends of Japan House Gallery

*Mrs. Vincent Astor
*Mr. and Mrs. Douglas Auchincloss
 Mrs. Harold L. Bache
*Mr. and Mrs. Armand P. Bartos
*Mr. Joe Brotherton
*Mr. and Mrs. Jackson Burke
*Mrs. Cornelius Crane
 Mr. and Mrs. Edgar Cullman, Jr.
 Mr. and Mrs. Lewis B. Cullman
 Mr. and Mrs. Richard M. Danziger
*Mr. and Mrs. C. Douglas Dillon
*Mr. and Mrs. Peter F. Drucker
 Mrs. Richard Ellis
*Mr. and Mrs. Myron S. Falk, Jr.
*Mr. Charles A. Greenfield
*Mr. Louis W. Hill, Jr.
*Mr. and Mrs. William H. Johnstone
*Mr. Yale Kneeland, III
*Mrs. Yale Kneeland, III
 Mrs. H. Irgens Larsen
*Mrs. Louis V. Ledoux
*Mr. and Mrs. Henry A. Loeb
*Mr. Stanley J. Love
 Mr. and Mrs. Richard D. Lombard
 Mr. and Mrs. C. Richard MacGrath
 Mr. and Mrs. Perry R. Pease
*Mr. and Mrs. Joe D. Price
*Mrs. John D. Rockefeller 3rd
*Mrs. Aye Simon
*Mr. and Mrs. Donald B. Straus
*Mrs. Arnold L. van Ameringen
 Mr. Henry P. van Amerigen
*Mr. Richard W. Weatherhead
*Miss Lucia Woods   *Founder

Officers of Japan Society, Inc.

Mr. John D. Rockefeller 3rd, Chairman of the Board
Mr. James M. Voss, Vice Chairman of the Board
Mr. Isaac Shapiro, President
Mr. Edgar B. Young, Vice President
Mr. Charles R. Stevens, Secretary
Mr. Tristan E. Beplat, Treasurer
Mr. David MacEachron, Executive Director

Advisory Committee on Arts

Mr. Arthur Drexler
Mr. William S. Lieberman
Dr. Murase Miyeko
Dr. John Rosenfield
Dr. Harold P. Stern

Committee on Care and Handling

Mr. Abe Mitsuhiro
Mr. Iguchi Yasuhiro
Mr. Sugiura Takashi

Catalogue designed by Kiyoshi Kanai
Photographs by Vincent Miraglia &
The Museum of Modern Art
Composition by Franklin Typographers, Inc., New York
Printed by Sterling-Roman Press, Inc., New York